ALL MY YESTERDAYS

Poems by

Mel Goldberg

ISBN: 978-81-19228-03-4

First Edition: 2023
Rs. 200/-

Cyberwit.net
HIG 45 Kaushambi Kunj, Kalindipuram
Allahabad - 211011 (U.P.) India
http://www.cyberwit.net
Tel: +(91) 9415091004
E-mail: info@cyberwit.net

Printed at VCORE.

ACKNOWLEDGEMENTS

First Fish

ASCENT ASPIRATIONS, 2016

The Deported Veteran Meets an Anglo Woman

Seven Hills Review, 2019

Goldfish Surgery

Lighten Up (UK Online) 2020

Contents

ALL MY YESTERDAYS

I may eat only rice and beans in my tortillas
and I will never forget
the days contemplating
our future as we hiked through
Arizona's the red rocks
and laughed as we stood at each vortex

I may be unable to drink tequila
but I will never forget
the wine you spilled
on our first night together
or the warmth of your naked body
on cold nights in the tent
before hiking in the snow
at Grand Canyon's North Rim

I may someday be unable to drive
but I will never forget driving
up to Moraine Lake in a blizzard
wondering if our old car would make it
but pushing on anyway to
the still lake that mirrored the mountains
or leaving Alaska in September
just ahead of the winter snow
and arriving at campgrounds
a day before they closed for the season.

I may need hearing aids and glasses
to survey all my yesterdays

but I will watch birds splashing in the fountain
and wave at boats on Lago de Chapala
as the winter days warm into spring

AN ATTACK OF POETRY

How can people who do not
read or write poetry
understand that
in the middle of the night
I may suddenly arise,
run to my desk,
and finding no paper,
begin writing on my arm,
over veins and hair,
starting at the elbow
and continuing to the wrist.

Exhausted when I return to bed,
my artist partner wakes, and smiles,
looks at my arm,
and does not ask questions.

BAKING BREAD

Knead the dough
until it is smooth,
slightly tacky to the touch,
and place it lovingly
into the oven.
Bake until golden brown,
crisp on the outside
with a touch of truth within.
so every bite
will fill the eater with surprise.

BALANCE

Thoth, Egyptian god of knowledge
with the head of an ibis
weighs every heart
to see if it will balance a feather.
For seventy years I studied books,
gathering more knowledge than I could use
in ten lifetimes.
Now, near the end, I understand
all that was needed I had in my heart
from the beginning.

PATIENCE

Trying to understand is like straining through muddy water.

Be still and allow the mud to settle.

Lao Tzu

I planted the small seed
of a Chinese bamboo tree,
watered it each day, gave it food
and watched, begging it to grow,
to send a tiny shoot
above the earth to let me know it lives.
I threatened it, "Look how the other plants have grown.
If you refuse to grow, I'll dig you up
and throw you in the trash!" But nothing worked.
I sought advice from an old sage
who spoke Chinese. He told the seed
the time had come to grow an inch.
But his words and my toil produced no benefit.
He said I must have patience.
A year passed by, and then another.
I forgot the tiny seed, having a life to live
A third year came. One day in the autumn
I looked out at my yard and saw a bamboo tree
that reached some five feet toward the sky.

THE BEST DAYS

The best days were walks
along the beach gathering shells
and watching starfish in tidepools
before we went for tacos and ice cream.
The walks welded us
stronger at the fused points,
pieces of steel that will never break.
Now I think of the ocean and cry
so happy to have had that time.

THE BOBCAT

On our hike
a bobcat stood
in the snow covered path.
I stopped and pointed.
"Look at that," I whispered to my
ten year old son. Awed, he stared at
tufted ears and tawny fur
slightly ruffled in the breeze,
like waves of water
undulating toward shore.
The bobcat stood majestic, graceful,
poised for flight at our slightest move.
His nose twitched, telling him
we were human, not food, not threat.

Three transient comrades on the trail.

LOOKING FOR A NEW DAY

Cold hovers in Chicago passageways
between the low brick houses,
and the oil-burning stove
tries to warm the pale green room.
My Sheffield mum sets her book on the table,
smells the burnt potatoes
and hurries to the stove
to turn off the fire under the copper pot
whose water has boiled away.

Short and plump, she walks to the window,
in the hazy glow of a table lamp,
a well-worn sweater over her soiled apron and flowered print dress,
looking for my father, whose penchant for gambling
often meant an empty-handed return from work.
She stares toward the endless sea of tenements
wondering what this night will bring,
a prisoner of a familiar routine
that now passes for life.

Thinking about ill fitting windows
and threadbare carpets,
leaking pipes and creaking floors,
she smiles, hums a childhood lullaby
heard only by the mice,
thinks about a youth
across the sea, and welcomes darkness.

LOVE MEANS SMILING

Love means smiling
when I help you change your shirt
stiff with the morning's food.
You have slipped back
eighty years
to be a child again
looking at life with wonder
asking me how the mountains got there.
We move slowly to the car
your feet unsure on the stones
forgetting they once climbed ladders
as surely as one born to heights.
I hold you by the arm
as we enter the same restaurant
where we have eaten for many months
and the waitress holds the door
smiles at me and nods.
Tears grace the corners of her eyes
as she brings your favorite breakfast -
a waffle covered with ice cream
chocolate syrup, and whipped cream.
I smile as I watch you pour maple syrup
on the top and eat the whole thing.

MOVING ON

I am slipping into September
as red and gold leaves of elms point the way.
I planned to organize the junk drawer
in the kitchen, the one where I keep
my pencils and paper,
but they have grown too large and heavy
and I am afraid I can no longer lift them.
My neighbors complain my yard is filled with weeds.
The wires sag under the weight of birds
There is a thin layer of dust
on my table, but I refuse to notice.
Tomorrow I may begin to sort through ideas
stored in the trunk in my basement,
but I know once I go down there
I shall never return

SILENT WALLS

Hundreds of feet below me, the Verde River
wanders through the canyon, as it did
a thousand years ago, when Old Ones
thrived among these cliffs. Through prickly pear
and yucca, I scoot down-hill,
grasping trunks of Palo Verde for support.
Stones click warnings as they fall away.
At last I stand before the ancient structure
built below the overhanging cliff.
Now hills and rocks glow in the evening sun
in rusty Anasazi hues of desiccated blood.
Touching my forehead to a rough hewn stone,
I smell the dust of empty centuries.
There is a presence here. The corner of my mind
detects a movement. I hear children's laughter.
Families, warmed by fire, eat meals
of venison and maize.
I seek wisdom in the woven straw
and clay that marks Hisotsinam design.
I listen, but the walls maintain their silence,
or whisper in a long forgotten tongue
known only to Massa'o and the wind.

YESTERDAY

In July
we faced the world naked
and skinny-dip[ped
in the cold mountain pool
while ripples played tag
with the sun through the dogwood.

I ran from the water
and put on everyone's clothes?
easily, effortlessly,
until I could hardly move.

Now in December
I watch the sun set on a lake
gripped by the fist of winter
where immobilized waves
help me remember
that I was once agile.

DISNEYLAND

The greasy hamburgers
were six dollars each,
and we watched people
waiting an hour
for the one-minute ride.
In shops we paid exorbitant prices
for mementos from China
that we lost in a month
but it was their childhood,
this bawdy house of fake fun;
I must seize the illusion
before it disappears.
Tinkerbell may glide on a wire
from the lighted castle
but maybe, just maybe
other children will make a wish
on that shooting star
before they disappear.

ELIMINATION

First I threw away adjectives
which are like fog
blotting out the hills and valleys.
Next I got rid of images because
winter is not at all like death,
and love is not a red, red, rose.
I eliminated *now* and *then*
to let everything happen
at the same time.
But I kept memory
although it was unreliable
and took looking backward
as my subject.
I was in love, once, I think,
a long time ago
in spring or summer

FIRST FISH

From the boat dock
my seven-year-old daughter,
barefoot in a tee shirt and shorts,
casts a line into the water
and catches her first fish.
I net the fish,
and put it, flopping,
into our pail filled with water.
She asks, "What if
it's some mommy fish's daughter?"

She throws her hands in the air
and shakes her head.
I turn to our bait bucket
and look back, smiling,
in time to see her grab the fish
and throw it back.

GLYPHS

Gregory loved hieroglyphs
He imagined himself
as an ancient man
in a loincloth
seated cross-legged
with a blank stone tablet
on his lap taking a sharp tool
and a small hammer
and chiseling pictographs.
He met a girl
and started thinking of her
in terms of glyphs.
A glyph for happiness
when they were together
and another for sadness
when they were apart.
Her scent in bed
became a glyph
and her kiss
became a glyph.
And when they parted,
he knew he had become a glyph.

EACH THING

Each thing is a whole,
random shapes
touching edge to edge.
Poems may be carved in stone
but the crow cries,
"You know. You know."
Leaves wave at stars
and the canyons are covered in snow
as yesterday's moon
stumbles over roofs,
peeks in cracks between rocks
and hallows the silver light of evening
in a global cooling of the heart.

WINTER SOLSTICE

Slowly the day
becomes visible
and the cold morning rises
over Lake Chapala
at the end of December.
the shortest day of the year,
as Earth continues its orbit
around the Sun.
Over sleeping houses
clouds create a winter prison
from which
the town noisily escapes.

Death whispers to me
from the shadows
telling me what I have become
and what I have not.

But I respond that
this is also the time of rebirth
signaling the beginning
of the lengthening of days.

BARKING DOGS

I listen to my dogs barking
and I wonder if they understand
when they hear other dogs bark.
Do they send signals
misunderstood by humans?
When a large black Lab
wandered into the yard,
my little chihuahua growled, barked,
and ran at the big dog
who tucked his tail and ran away,
which I suppose was a dog apology
a way of saying, "I'm sorry,
I know that is your space,"
I understood the woman who bumped into me
with her cart at the market
and said "Excuse me."
But maybe I need a doggie translator
to tell them I do not like being watched
when I am showering or sitting on the toilet

END OF THE YEAR

The year is ending
when all the world must pause
Yet underneath the frozen lake
life moves beneath the ice.

So trilobites
compressed into the earth
millions of years ago, greet us
with messages, their history revealed
in stone and shale.

Soldiers who sleep
beneath their monuments of time
warn those of us who wait
for yet another day
to finish tasks undone.

I went to Stratford to commemorate
the birth of William Shakespeare,
put flowers on his tomb,
stood near the altar in the church
and recalled Hamlet's words
about the undiscovered country
"from whose bourne
no traveller returns" or miserable Macbeth's,
who mused that "all our yesterdays have lighted fools
The way to dusty death."

Endings teach that time, relentless,
carries on unseen into a future
where we'll be unremembered
save in what we leave behind

I AM NOT AFRAID OF DEATH

although it is the defining moment
that tells me what I had become
and what I had not.

I am not afraid of death
who holds the hourglass
of sand that cannot be stopped.

I am not afraid of death
yet he is the sorcerer
who will make my body vanish,
while my name may be engraved
temporarily in hearts.

I am angered by death
because he will cause pain,
an emptiness in the loved ones
I leave behind

I WANT TO AGE

I want to age
like an old house in winter
with friends sitting around the fireplace
sharing stories, sipping kahlúa and coffee
safe from the snow and cold.

I want to age like a redwood
growing stronger every year
telling history in the rings.

I want to age like the Niobrara
calm and shallow but deep enough
to float canoes and kayaks
flowing around timeless bends.

I want to age like Mount Shasta
with trails and secret caves,
ancient and snow topped.

I want to age like the moon
lighting the night sky in reflected glory
disappearing slowly from full to new
until I am no longer there

LOSS

I hike down into Grand Canyon
from the from the South Rim
on the Bright Angel Trail
carrying my 5 year old son
on my back. The stillness
of the morning echoes in our ears.
The poem does not start here.

At a turn on the switchback trail
he loses one of his favorite hiking boots.
This is still not the beginning
and only a family
can understand the loss.

You may know of the horror
of Zika virus or count the bodies
after a terrorist shooting
so the small loss of a shoe
may seem insignificant

but he has walked through mud
after a rain in these shoes
and they were special hiking shoes.

Although he has other shoes,
he is unconsoled and says
he will be unable to hike
without them.

So I retrace my steps
and ask returning hikers
"Have you seen a small hiking boot?"
They all answer, "Sorry, no."

I return to camp in silence
my hands empty as an abandoned
hawk's nest. Still the poem has not started.

The next day I drive into Flagstaff
with my son's surviving boot
and ask at the Boot Barn
if anyone can find a mate for the shoe
and the manager says, "Yes,
I also have a five-year-old son."

Now the poem starts,
my joy will echo in the air
and my song on a flute made from
the hollow branch of a tree
will pierce the sky.

TWO MOONS

What if the earth
had two moons
always full, rising together
like two eyes in the night sky
bright enough to read and write poetry.
Yet maybe this would be
more than we want
for two lovers might be
walking along the moonlit beach
hand in hand
while he looks at one moon
and she looks at the other

WHAT SONG WILL I SING

The past years have become
stacked boards leaning against the wind.
What song will I sing at the end
when I know I shall never return
when I watch the earth fall away
as my soul climbs toward the unknown?
When it is clear I shall never again
see the sunset
casting long shadows over the city
Or watch the full moon
rising in the night sky.
What will wait for me
when I slip
singing into the darkness.

THE DANGER OF BUTTERFLIES

I am wary of creatures that look attractive,
but may harbor a hidden peril.
I have been fooled by the graceful bodies
of humans whose allure masked
a capricious nature and a callous lack of compassion.
Butterflies are beautiful
and therefore may be dangerous,
like the African Giant Swallowtail,
the most toxic of the species.
with enough poison to kill a cat.
They are solitary flyers and spread pollen
but colonies of bees do it far better.
Perhaps butterflies envy the bees' society
and their ability to build hives and create honey.
Yet deception may have an evolutionary purpose
like the toxic Viceroy butterfly
which is very similar to the larger monarch.
Or mosquitoes that need only a drop of blood to survive.
The female praying mantis bites off her partner's head
during sex and her action has become synonymous
with a *femme fatale*, whose beauty ensnares lovers.

THE DEAD MAY RETURN

The dead may return to you in dreams
or when you are awake, they will be cats
scratching at the door wanting a way in.
The dead will speak as the wind,
leaves of trees will be their tongues.
The dead will never leave you
their unrest will be the coat
you wear in winter to shield you
from the cold and if you ignore them
they will be offended.
They will require an accounting,
demanding everything
but once you give all you have
they will tell you it is not enough.

MAXWELL STREET

Just south of the downtown area,
past the University of Illinois/Chicago,
past streets named for presidents,
Van Buren, Harrison, Taylor,
past Roosevelt Road,
exists Chicago's famous Maxwell Street,
hundreds of stalls, lean-tos, tents squeezed tight,
all manned by immigrants - mostly Jews
from Poland, Germany, Hungary,
who had escaped the European hatred.
You could buy anything from a clawfoot tub,
to a lawnmower or computer,
to a motorcycle without a motor,
to a tattered copy of *Leaves of Grass*
bound in Naugahyde and all
with prices that could be negotiated
by pretending disinterest.

So what drew us in our youth
to walk five miles on Sunday
to this place that seemed
magical and enchanting?
None of us were bargain hunters or hoarders.
We were Jewish kids in worn jeans
and chinos, with threadbare jackets,
pockets with barely with enough money
to buy hot dogs or hoagies and cokes.

We came to squeeze a little joy
from the lemon dregs of our destiny,
like pilgrims attracted to a shrine.

Now as Jewish adults
we walk the same streets talking, joking,
oblivious to time and space,
joining the crowds milling about
but we do not care, for once again
we feel alive with every breath,
every word, every thought that brings us back
to our stubborn youth when we were seeds
about to grow into men and fool the world.

YESTERDAYS FALL AWAY

Yesterdays fall away
like pages torn from
a lose leaf notebook
carried by the air.
They float away
and although I run after them
and put my foot on one
I am too slow
and watch those endless days
flying away
like evenings with friends
at the ocean beach.
The salty air
hides my tears.

GOLDFISH SURGERY

No one does surgery
on a goldfish.
When I had surgery and
went under the anesthetic
I imagined it was like dying
like when my two pet goldfish sank
and were motionless
in the bottom of their tank.
I read that the oldest goldfish
on record lived to be 43,
which is exactly half my age.
I thought about taking them
to the veterinarian and
imagined a nurse in a white coat
holding a mini-stethoscope
against their little chests,
and a doctor writing
a prescription for pills
to make them well.
I would like to have asked them
if they were puzzled about
their limited world with
the green rocks and the castle
and what they understood
about life and death,
and if they were more intuitive
than we are

THE DEPORTED VETERAN MEETS AN ANGLO WOMAN

You look like a nice gringa lady.

I was born in this neighborhood
a few blocks from here.
You're an Estadounidensay, aren't you?
that's someone from United States.
I used to get tortillas at Maria's Tortilleria
That's on Broadway near Swan Road
twenty years ago when I lived in Tucson
before I volunteered.

When I was a kid, my mama'd send me
to get *cordero* at Antonio's Meat Market
over on Hidalgo Street not far from here
in La Floresta. It ain't there anymore. Nothing is.
The lamb was chewy. And my mama cooked it
well done with frijoles the way my papa liked it.

I was cute then. Black hair to go with my dark skin.
"Negruzco" they called me. Hard to believe, eh lady?
Now I sleep in the arroyos at night under the bridge
and mostly wash cars to make a few pesos.

Then they deported me, got no papers they said
when they picked me up for DUI
except my discharge papers after two years in Iraq.

I really need a beer and an empanada.
I usually go to El Barco when I get money.
It's on the Carretera near Pancho's.

El Barco is a dive, but the Corona
goes for only 20 pesos.

Did I tell you I write poetry? Did I tell you that?
In English and Spanish
I'm not just your ordinary Mexican, I'm a poet.
You think *esta uno broma*, it's a joke?
If you come back here tomorrow,
I'll give you a poem and prove it.
I read a lot of poetry
and spend most of my days
at the American Legion,
down on Morelos in Chapala.
Its quiet there, and sometimes Miguel treats me
to a taco or two at the bar.

You come back and I'll have your poem in my pocket.
It won't be as depressing as Federico Méndez
but less stiff than Garcia Lorca
and just as pretentious as Octavio Paz.

CHINESE LUNAR ROVER FINDS *GEL-LIKE* SUBSTANCE

When I read the Chinese Land Rover
had discovered a gel-like substance
on the far side of the moon,
it made me remember when I was in high school
and a movie *The Blob*, that Steve McQueen flick
where a gelatinous substance consumed
and subsumed suburban people in dark alleys
and movie theaters, before being airlifted
to the azure ice of the Arctic, where I figure
it mutated and found its way to the Antarctic
and somehow became *The Thing*.
Most girls successfully avoided me,
with sudden interest in ceiling architecture
as I passed them in the hallways
with my saturnine, hopelessly hopeful eyes.
I think about the girls I took to a movie
back in those horrifying years,
those Chicago teenage beauties with their big hair
held together by gallons of hair gel and
a pick that looked like a Jason Voorhees weapon
turning five-foot girls
into leggy Geena Davis, who starred in *The Fly*,
another example of science causing trouble.
There was a moment when I snaked my arm
around a girl's shoulder and surreptitiously dropped my hand
down toward her breast and my finger caught, glued by the gel,
like some hapless fly trapped in the viscous web of a spider.
The girls' gelled hair often bumped up against the roofs

of my friends' cars, so after a date or two
large round greasy circles appeared.
Sitting under one of these globular blobs
was like sitting under an oily moon,
with its dark side gel the Chinese discovered.

I think I speak for the entire world when I say
please leave that jellylike shit where you found it.
Some things are better left where they are,
be they found on the moon or in the past.
No need to discover new veins of sorrow.
Steve McQueen is dead, Geena Davis
drove over that cliff with Susan Sarandon,
even The Thing would prefer to go back to sleep.
I know that after four or five decades
almost all of those once achingly beautiful girls
avoid their mirrors like they once avoided me.

SKY BLUE CAMRY

The summer after high school we did nothing
except steal fruit from outside bins at neighborhood
stores—plums from Hoffmann's, cherries from A & P,
grapefruits from Krogers for throwing from
Billy's fifth floor balcony. Some of us
were going to college but most of us
weren't. We skateboarded along flat LaSalle Street
under the ninety-degree sun, the kind of sun
that made us run after the ice truck.
We skated on the steps behind at the Fourth Presbyterian
until the pastor chased us away. David was the best
among us, would do things I was too scared to do.
He landed a switch frontside flip off a nine-stair,
and if you know what that means you know
it is something to see. One night David threw a party
at his house—his parents didn't care
about alcohol. For no apparent reason
a girl named Lauren led me by the hand
to the garage, put her arms around my neck,
and stuck her tongue in my mouth.
I was thinking I'd finally stumbled onto some luck
but when I slid my hand under the waistband
of her dress and touched her skin,
she pulled away and said people will know.
No one else is here in the garage I said, but it was clear
she'd made up her mind. So we sat on the floor and talked
about what we planned to do in the future.
When we heard screeching tires out front,

we ran and there in the middle of the street
was a sky-blue Toyota Camry, like the one my uncle had.

A middle-aged woman stepped out and
looked under her car where she saw David
not moving, his neck twisted at a strange angle.
The woman kept forking her fingers
through her hair, and she kept silently
opening and closing her mouth
like a fish. Days later when the autopsy came back
we learned that before being run over
David already died of a heroin overdose, right there
in the street. Maybe he'd been looking up
at the stars as the drug gently coaxed him
to stop breathing. I still think of that poor woman
in the sky-blue Camry and the nights
she must have spent thinking she
had killed David before finding out she'd just
run over something that was already dead.

A BIRD FLIES INTO MY WINDOW

As I started to eat dinner
I heard a thump and saw a large bird
had flown into my patio window
hard enough to shatter the glass
and land inside on the floor.
The injustice of glass is
civilization with a view.
The dead bird lay amid the shards
and I found an old shoe box,
filled with wrinkled tissue paper
and put in the hapless bird.
as I pondered my own mortality.
There is humility in cleaning
up broken glass as I gathered the pieces
and put them in the box with the bird.

LETTER TO MY FATHER 20 YEARS AFTER HIS DEATH

You should know that small plane rides
over Lake Michigan regularly happen
and Navy Pier still smells
like peanuts and cotton candy.
You would be happy to know
that I visited the old house on Crilly Court
where you first told me about
hitchhiking across the country,
to look for work when you were nineteen,
painting signs for food and lodging
You gave up painting signs
after Parkinson's had frozen your hands.
Grief creates moments that catch in my throat
like hearing your old corny joke:
on the other hand she wore a glove.
I think of you when I make coffee each morning
and watch for ravens in trees
to deliver your message from the other side.
I kept the cup I gave you
that says "World's Greatest Dad,"
the handle no longer sticky from the honey
you used in your coffee.
I held your hand in mine
as you took your last breath.
The sharp edges of that moment cut me
but they have become
rounded with memory.

I guess it comes down to timing.
You loved to see
the morning light reflected from the lake
but you said the show must go on.
So does the emptiness.

ROMEO AND JULIET TEN YEARS LATER

When Nietsche was asked
the best thing a man could do,
he said "Never to be born.
And the second is to die young."
An example is Romeo and Juliet.
But what if they had not succumbed
to the poison, had lived and married,
and their families, having worked out
their differences, had become friends.
Ten years later the two lovers
now have three kids and Juliet,
having gained thirty pounds,
stays home cleaning and cooking
while Romeo, his paunch hanging
over his belt sash and looking more like
Falstaff than a handsome Montague,
is drinking in the pub with his friends
Mercutio and Benvolio.
Nietsche died of pneumonia at fifty-six
complicated by dementia.

THE GATHERING

Three crows gather
on the fence behind my house
I am startled by their shiny black beauty
so discordant with their raucous voices.
They hop from one foot to the other
restless as if hesitant to report
from the other side to tell me
of souls who want to return.

They miss the sunshine
on a summer afternoon
the shimmer of the moon
on the sea
or a cold beer after working
outside on a hot day.

The crows watch me as I sit and write
at my computer on my patio.
and nod their heads
to remind me.

A BAG OF TRASH

A bag of trash ripped open
by some dogs reveals a life
in chicken bones, crusts of bread,
and a laceless tennis shoe
once loved and useful
now worn out like many of us,
discarded, no longer wanted.
Life is a series of eliminations
so when I take out a plastic bag
filled with debris and mistakes
I wonder if the bin is large enough

AFTER I DIE

I do not know what will happen
after I die. I have no answer
to the question or if my death
will be by disease or bullet.
But what if death turns out to be
thrilling and fun? Could there be
something somewhere where I will
see friends again? Will my
favorite song be stuck forever
in my head? Or will one medicine
prolong my life so I will wish
for another medicine to end it?
My cat brought in a dead mouse
with eyes vacant and unseeing as lead BBs
and I wondered if we are the only beings
with a recognition of death.
When I scuba dived in Hawaii, I swam
in awe near a whale. When I stood at the base
of the General Sherman Redwood Tree,
I experienced loneliness so profound
that my writing failed to capture it.
Is science or God keeping the scales in balance
or are they tipped toward unfairness
so we have an irrational fear of spiders
but experience butterflies as a form of pleasure?

HE WHO LAUGHS LAST

The man who laughs last
understands the deeper meaning
so if you laugh at yourself
you will become revered by others.
There is a sadness hidden in laughter.
and correctness with emotion
will cause fear among those hearing you.
But never allow yourself the easy path
of evasion and do nothing.
Horrible things occur
when people stand idly by.
If you believe fate
has given you one set of circumstances
and you think your job is to create another,
do not worry if you fail.
So much of importance has occurred by accident.
The Bible was written by people telling stories.
They did not think they were writing The Bible.

I AM LEARNING

I am learning to love myself
the way the shore loves the ocean
and accepts waves that diminish it.
I am learning to love my body
the way b's and d's are shaped
like the bellies of pregnant women
because everything I write is birth.
I am learning to love my name
even after I learned it was not my name
because my father had been adopted
and was given his step-father's name.
I am learning to love the warm sun
although I always consider
I have a limited number of days.
I am learning to love the night because
the moon climbs over the city
the way a reader waits for a story to build to a climax.
I am learning to love the future although
it may not be what I imagine it to be
because it is uncertain like opening my eyes
in the dark room of forgiveness
and receiving what I have not earned.
I am learning to love life
and although I think about death
I will not be saddened.

MY VIOLIN

As a young man,
when I resined my bow
and tucked my violin
beneath my chin to play,
I moved into a place
without pain, my playing
a defense against the world.
Guitar players thought it strange
to have a fingerboard without frets.
They did not understand
when my fingers teased a vibrato,
I entered deep into the mystery of music,
the hidden rooms only I could enter.

THE ELK TREE

I lived in a house near Flagstaff
for ten years caring for the apple
tree in the front yard.
Each year I looked forward
to ripe apples in September
but I never got to eat any.
I named it the Elk Tree
because a herd of Roosevelt Elk
lived in the forest near the house.
After the blossoms dropped in spring
an elk would wander by each day
to inspect the tree for apples.
Imagine members of the local herd
questioning the designated inspector.
When the apples showed a blush of red
the herd would come by - mothers
standing on hind legs to reach high branches
and young ones eating the low hanging fruit.
They left partially eaten apples under the tree.
Imaging them each evening, bellies full
laughing and chatting, telling human jokes,
leaving no apples for me.

THE RED BEAST

I called it "The Red Beast,"
a 1939 Buick Coupe
with a straight eight
that would do an easy eighty
on any open road.
Wearing no mask, I sprayed it
fire-engine red and sneezed
red for a week.
It was fourteen years old
when I bought it, just
three years younger than I,
and thinking about it now
in the highway of my mind,
we are young again, the car
and the 80-year-old man,
both remnants of the 50s
wanting a Mulligan.
a do-over, unwilling
to say good-bye to our yesterdays.

HUMMINGBIRD FEEDER

I had a hummingbird feeder
filled with sugar water
but I took it down because
they all fought for a place
and at night the bats would come
which caused my dogs to bark.
But near my patio, on a low branch,
I saw a tiny nest of twigs
and shredded leaves with
a thimble-size egg that would someday
be a beautiful hummingbird.
Ornithologists worry that some birds
may become extinct, like
peregrine falcons or turkey vultures.
I do not want creatures who defy gravity
to disappear but chittering reminds me
of the problem with human nature
and its constant inability to secure
a place at nature's table.
Perhaps humans are just a blip
on the evolutionary scale like
the dodo bird or the black rhinoceros,
and will disappear because they never
learned to share and became devoted to
gathering and hoarding, conspicuous consumption,
indoor toilets, heating, and air-conditioning.

MUSIC OF THE HEART

What is the opposite of music? Silence of death.
- Volodomyr Zelensky

The shallow Niobrara River
has the cadence of moving water
as I step in it to steady my canoe,
and it reverberates over my legs
creating a dance of waves
that moves in crests and troughs
like an electrocardiogram
recording the music of the heart.
It rises and falls when we sing
in joy or in grief,
a survival mechanism
against the evil of the world.
that has been recorded
in Armenia, in Auschwitz,
in Croatia, in Ukraine,
where people are suspended
between life and death,
lifted only by song,
an electrocardiogram
that measures the music
of the world's heart.

That steady rhythm
is what we hold on to,
like the flow of a river
moving in a dance of waves

under a cloudy sky,
a sound loud enough
to drown the silence the grave.

www.ingramcontent.com/pod-product-compliance
Lightning Source LLC
LaVergne TN
LVHW040959150826
845672LV00002B/766

* 9 7 8 8 1 1 9 2 2 8 0 3 4 *